MINI MEDITATIONS ON

CREATIVITY

Tillie Walden

First published in 2018 by Liminal 11

Images copyright © 2018 Tillie Walden

Illustrated by Tillie Walden

All rights reserved. No part of this publication may be reproduced, stored in a retrieval system, or transmitted in any form or by any means, electronic, mechanical, photocopying, recording or otherwise, without written permission from the publisher.

Book design and colour by Mike Medaglia

Printed in Slovenia

ISBN 978-1-912634-01-9

10 9 8 7 6 5 4 3 2 1

www.liminal11.com

MINI MEDITATIONS ON

CREATIVITY

Tillie Walden

INTRODUCTION

If you do a Google Image search for 'creativity', almost every image that comes up is of a light bulb. This deeply bothers me. I know, I know, it's just Google Images, I shouldn't take this personally. Yet I do. Creativity, in my mind, is a very complex and nuanced concept. Creativity is everything, and it's everywhere. And despite its ubiquity it can still be maddeningly elusive when you need it most. It is so much more than the flash of a lightbulb.

When I started drawing this book, I had this in mind. I didn't want to illustrate a simplistic, overdone version of creativity. I wanted to tap into what it really means to be creative, what it means to fight with it and live with it and accept it. Being a creative person, in any respect, is often a struggle, and I specifically tried to seek out quotes and drawings for this book that addressed that. In my experience, it takes a lot more than just confidence or optimism to get you working on something that matters, something that truly has meaning to you.

What I think gets forgotten about in the conversation around creativity is the part of the equation where you have to work. Getting inspired is a beautiful thing, and this book can help to instil that in you, but nothing will come of it if you don't take that inspiration and do something with it. In my mind, that's often where the real endeavour is. That gap between what we conjure in our minds and what we actually do. It's something I still battle with, even as a professional artist and graphic novelist.

While I was drawing the pages for this little book, I was once again struck by a truth that I manage to forget every single time I have an idea. It feels good to make things. And it feels even better to finish them.

I hope in reading these quotes and seeing these drawings you can take some of that with you in your own creative life.

Tillie Walden

- Ernest J. Gaines

Inhale possibility, exhale creativity.

- Laura Jaworski

Inspiration is some mysterious blessing which happens when the wheels are turning smoothly.

- Quentin Blake

The days you work
are the best days.

-Georgia O'Keeffe

The scariest moment is always just before you start.

After that, things can only get better.

-Stephen King

Creativity is contagious, pass it on.

- Albert Einstein

The point about working is not to produce great stuff all the time, but to remain ready for when you can.

- Brian Eno

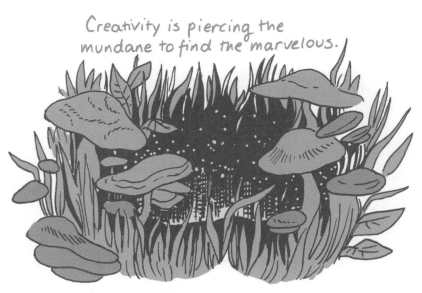

Creativity is piercing the mundane to find the marvelous.

~ Bill Moyers

You can't use up creativity.
The more you use, the more you have.

-Maya Angelou

Arrange whatever pieces
come your way.

-Virginia Woolf

I think each of us, sometime in our life, has wanted to paint a picture.

- Bob Ross

You can sit there, tense and worried, freezing the creative energies, or you can start writing something.

It doesn't matter what.

In 5 or 10 minutes, the imagination will heat, the tightness will fade, and a certain spirit and rhythm will take over.

— Leonard Bernstein

Creativity is the way I share my soul with the world.

— Brené Brown

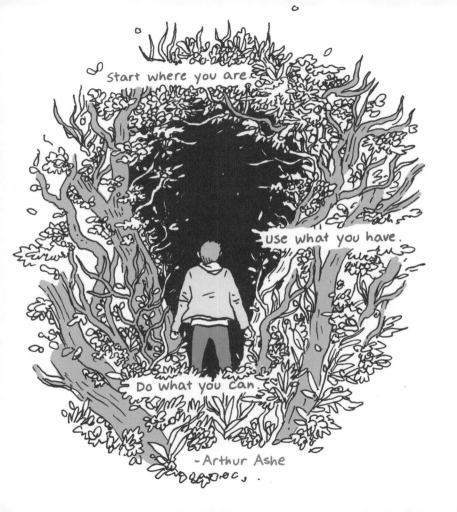

Great things are not done by impulse,
but by a series of small things brought together.

-Vincent Van Gogh

Passion is one great force that unleashes creativity, because if you're passionate about something, then you're more willing to take risks.

- Yo-Yo Ma

Action may not always bring happiness

but there is no happiness without action.

-Benjamin Disraeli

Beyond talent lie all the usual words:
discipline, love, luck — but, most of all,
endurance.

-James Baldwin

Creativity is more than just being different. Anybody can plan weird; that's easy.

What's hard is to be as simple as Bach. Making the simple, awesomely simple, that's creativity.

—Charles Mingus

— Gloria E. Anzaldúa

The world always seems brighter
    when you've just made something
        that wasn't there before.

        - Neil Gaiman

— Melody Ross

If you hear a voice within you say 'you cannot paint,' then by all means *paint* and that voice will be silenced.

-Vincent Van Gogh

Creating means living.

- Dejan Stojanovic

Also in the Mini Meditations series:

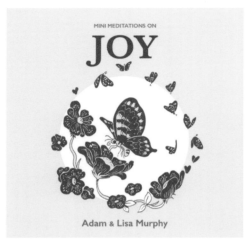

Bursting with positivity and bliss,
Mini Meditations on Joy is sure to inspire
the delight within!

ISBN: 978-1-912634-02-6

light at the crossroads